go for it!

inspiring words of determination

edited by jo ryan

Published in the United States in 2005
by Tangent Publications
an imprint of
Axis Publishing Limited
8c Accommodation Road
London NW11 8ED
www.axispublishing.co.uk

Creative Director: Siân Keogh
Editorial Director: Anne Yelland
Production Manager: Jo Ryan

ISBN 1–904707–23–8

2 4 6 8 10 9 7 5 3 1

Printed and bound in China

go for it!

about this book

A collection of thoughts and sayings on the value of trying as a means of succeeding, *Go For It!* is a celebration of effort, determination, tenacity, perseverance, and hard work. Contrary to what most people feel, the majority of successful people aren't simply lucky—they have made their own luck through hard work and never giving up, no matter how insurmountable a problem seemed. These words of wisdom are designed to pick people up when they have been dealt a blow, lead them on when they want to stand still, and push them forward when they want to shrink back.

Complemented by gently amusing animal photographs, the thoughts and sayings here will inspire anyone to do and be their best, whatever their individual circumstances.

about the author

Jo Ryan is an editor and author who has been involved in publishing books and magazines across a range of subjects for several years. From the many hundreds of contributions that were sent to her, she has selected the ones that best sum up the value of carrying on trying through life's ups and downs, trials and tribulations.

Waste your money and you've only wasted money…

…waste your time and you've lost part of your life.

When all is said and
done a lot more will have
been said than done.

Success is making the best possible use of what you have been given.

You can't leave footprints
in the sands of time
if you're sitting on
your butt. And who
wants to leave buttprints
in the sands of time?

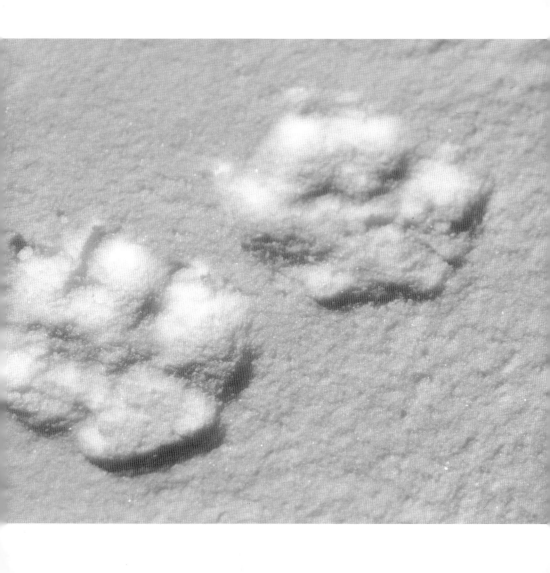

All that stands between
the graduate and the top of
the ladder is the ladder.

You don't have to stay up nights to achieve success—you need to stay awake days.

Dreams are like stars…

…you can't touch them,
but you can follow them to
your destiny.

Many people have gone
further than they thought
they could because
someone else thought
they could.

The only way to see a rainbow
is to look through the rain.

The harder you fall,
the higher you bounce.

There is room at the top,
but nowhere to sit.

Success is the ability to do better than good enough.

If you refuse to accept anything
but the best, you'll get the best.

No dream is ever too big, and no dreamer is ever too small.

People don't only
succeed through success;
they often succeed
through failures.

The best way out of a difficulty is through it.

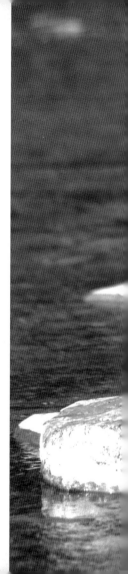

Don't ask for a light
load: ask instead
for a strong back.

The secret of success
is to do everything
you can without
thinking about success.

If at first you don't succeed, reboot.

Happiness is not doing what you like, but liking what you must do.

You can't turn back the clock,
but you can wind it up again.

If you look for rest,
you'll find boredom…

…if you look for work,
you'll find rest.

Admit your mistakes—
before somebody else
exaggerates them.

It's humiliating to
make a mistake…

…but it's even worse
if nobody notices.

The only real mistake
is not learning from
your mistakes.

If the going is easy,
take care: you may be
headed downhill.

Never say "Oops."
Always say
"Ah, interesting."

Success is building
the foundations with
the bricks other
people throw at you.

It's not because things are difficult that we don't dare…

…it's because we don't dare that things are difficult.

The only way to escape criticism: do nothing, say nothing, be nothing.

Obstacles: those things you see when you take your eyes off your goals.

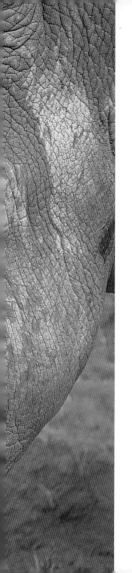

If you can't go around,
or over, or through it,
you're going to have
to negotiate with it.

Some people make
it happen, others watch
it happen, and some say,
"What happened?"

If you're not sure where you're going, you'll probably end up somewhere else.

Success happens in private, failure in public.

The way to do more
is not to think of
things as impossible.

Two wrongs are only
the beginning.

Nearly all men can stand adversity, but if you want to test a man's character, give him power.

A big shot is a little shot
who kept shooting.

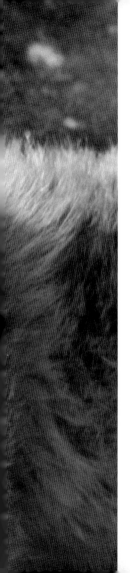

Happiness is dreaming
dreams, and working
to make them
come true.

The mark of true
genius is originality.

People can because they think they can.

When opportunity
meets preparation,
success is the result.

Failure is only the opportunity to begin again, this time more wisely.

First build your castles in the air, then worry about the foundations.

There is a time to let things happen and a time to make things happen.

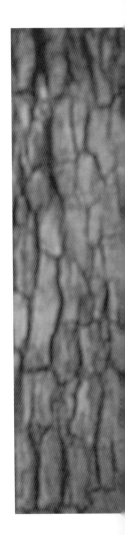

"I can't" never
accomplished anything…

…"I will try" has
worked wonders.

The greater the difficulty,
the more glory in
overcoming it.

There is no worth in anything that is not difficult to achieve.

Don't ask for tasks
equal to your powers…

…ask for powers
equal to your tasks.

Achieving is easiest when we work the hardest, and hardest when we work the easiest.

If Columbus had turned
back, no one would have
remembered him.

People who do things that count usually don't stop to count them.

It is better to live richly
than to die rich.

Success is open to everyone who chooses his goal and goes for it.

Don't wait for success…

…go ahead without it.

A success is a dreamer someone believed in.

People become great
by doing what they don't
want to do when they
don't want to do it.

Success isn't how far you've come, but how far you're from where you started.

Getting anywhere means
starting somewhere.